UNDERSTANDING DISEASE
ARTHRITIS

UNDERSTANDING DISEASE

ARTHRITIS

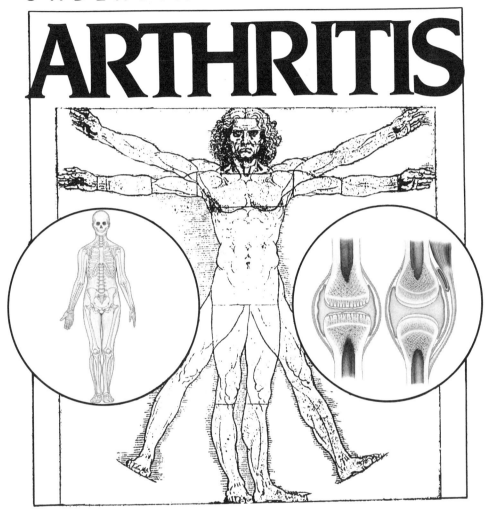

STEVEN TIGER

ILLUSTRATED BY MICHAEL REINGOLD

MEDICAL CONSULTANT: MICHAEL KATZ, M.D.

DIRECTOR, PEDIATRIC SERVICE, BABIES HOSPITAL COLUMBIA-PRESBYTERIAN MEDICAL CENTER, NEW YORK CITY

JULIAN MESSNER NEW YORK

Illustrations pages 45 and 47 courtesy Little, Brown from Primer of Clinical Radiology *by Thomas T. Thompson, M.D., Copyright 1980 by Little, Brown and Company Inc.*

Illustration page 44 courtesy W. B. Saunders Company from Synopsis of Radiologic Anatomy with Computed Tomography *by Isadore Mescham, M.A., M.D., Copyright 1980 by W. B. Saunders Company.*

Published by Julian Messner, A Division of Simon & Schuster, Inc. Simon & Schuster Building, Rockefeller Center, 1230 Avenue of the Americas, New York, New York 10020
JULIAN MESSNER and colophon are trademarks of Simon & Schuster, Inc.
Manufactured in the United States of America

Design by Linda Kosarin

10 9 8 7 6 5 4 3 2 1

Library of Congress Cataloging in Publication Data
Tiger, Steven.   Arthritis.
   Includes index.
   Summary: Describes how the bones and joints are put together, what goes wrong when there is arthritis, what causes it, and how it is treated.
   1. Arthritis – Juvenile literature.   [1. Arthritis]
I. Title.   II. Series.
RC933.T44 1985   616.7'22   85-8947
ISBN 0-671-55566-9

CONTENTS

1: WHAT IS ARTHRITIS?

Arthritis means "inflamed joint." *Arthron* is the Greek word for "joint," and *-itis* is from the Greek word for "inflammation." When the two parts of the word are put together, the last two letters of arthron are dropped. So arthr + itis = arthritis.

Arthritis is not a single disease. In fact, there are many different conditions that can be called arthritis. What do they have in common? Inflammation in the joints. Inflammation* is a condition that causes swelling, warmth, redness, and pain. Because inflammation is the

*Defined in the glossary

main feature in arthritis, we must learn a little about this process.

When body tissue becomes damaged, it has to be repaired. Inflammation is a process that takes place as the body repairs damaged tissues. The damaged cells spill out many substances. Some of these substances attract white blood cells from the bloodstream into the area of damage. These white blood cells clear away the bits of damaged tissue while healthy new cells grow in. As this work goes on, there is more blood flow in the area than normal, bringing in extra oxygen and nutrients to supply the repair process. This

7

increased blood flow causes warmth and redness. As fluid collects, there is swelling. Pain is caused by certain complex substances that are formed when cells are damaged. These substances, called prostaglandins*, make the nerves in the area very sensitive. In other parts of the body prostaglandins control blood pressure, intestinal muscles, glandular functions, and metabolism.

But if inflammation is a normal process that repairs damaged tissues, why is it a problem? It isn't – if it's normal. Problems occur if the damage continues, or if the inflammation itself causes damage. As we'll see, this is what happens in many forms of arthritis.

Some people use the word arthritis incorrectly. In fact, some people call any pain in the joints or bones arthritis, but that is wrong. A bone that is broken or infected causes pain, but that is not arthritis. The word *arthritis* should be used only for conditions in which there is inflammation in the joints. Another word that some people use for pain in the bones and joints is *rheumatism*. Doctors don't use this word, because it doesn't have an exact medical definition.

WHO GETS ARTHRITIS?

About 75 million people in the United States have pain in the bones or joints, at least sometimes – that is, about one out of every three Americans. In most cases, the pain is slight and it doesn't last long. But over 20 million people have worse pain that doesn't go away. It causes these people problems in moving, walking, or using their hands. They need medical treatment for pain and stiffness so that they can do their jobs and enjoy a normal life. Almost three million people have very bad pain and other problems from arthritis, even with treatment.

Anyone can get arthritis. Some people think that the disease only affects old people, but that is not true. Even children can get certain kinds of arthritis. Who is most likely to get arthritis? Four factors are important.

1. Age and sex. Some forms of arthritis are seen more often in one group of people than in another – for example, in women more often than in men. Some are more common in older people, while other forms are seen mainly in children.

2. Lifestyle. People who sit around all day are more likely to get certain kinds of arthritis than people who get lots of exercise.

Some kinds of arthritis affect women more than men. Other kinds affect men more often. And some kinds affect children.

And if an active person does get arthritis, it may be easier to treat the disease. But if a person injures a joint in an accident, arthritis may appear in the same joint years later. So exercise is good, but we have to be careful not to hurt ourselves.

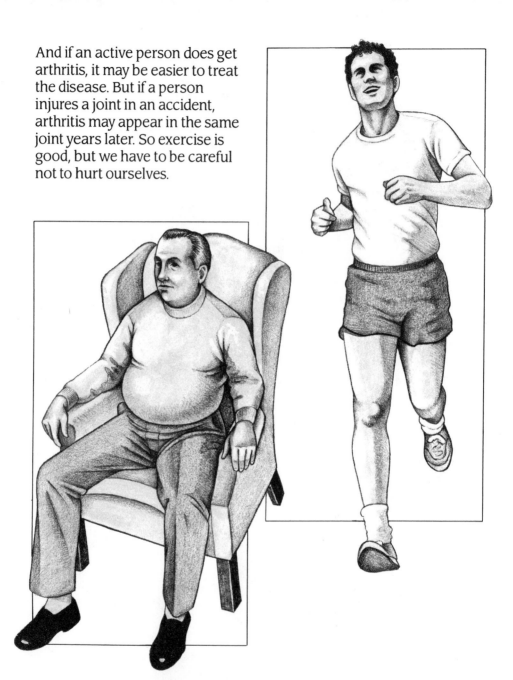

People who keep physically active are less likely to develop some kinds of arthritis. If they do develop it, the disease will not be as bad as in people who get no exercise.

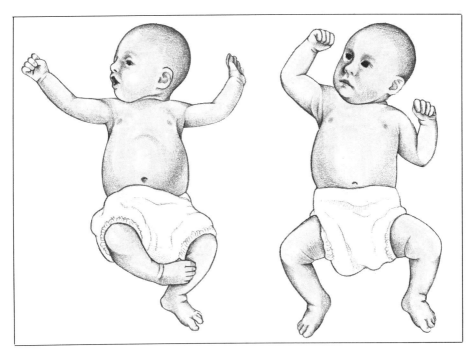

Some people are just born more likely to develop arthritis than other people.

3. Family history. Certain forms of arthritis tend to appear in many members of the same family. Someone who has lots of relatives with one form of arthritis is more likely to get that disease than a person who has no family history of arthritis.

4. Other diseases. People who get certain diseases of the intestines often get arthritis at about the same time. Doctors are trying to learn more about why this happens.

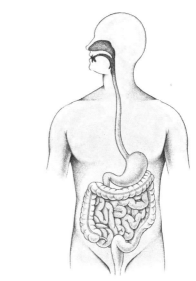

Certain diseases of the intestines seem often to appear with certain types of arthritis.

THE OUTLOOK FOR ARTHRITIS

Arthritis has been a problem throughout history. For a long time, people thought that nothing could be done for arthritis. But as we learn more and more about it, one thing becomes very clear: Arthritis can often be prevented – and even if a person does get arthritis, the disease can usually be treated very well and then the person can lead a normal, active life.

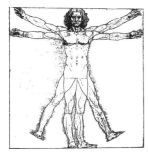

2: ABOUT BONES AND JOINTS

THE SKELETON

Have you ever seen a house being built? There is a framework of strong posts and beams that supports the walls and floors. Without that wood or metal framework, even a brick house could fall apart.

Inside the body, we also need a framework, and that is the skeleton. The human skeleton is made up of 206 connected bones. Without the skeleton, we would not be able to stand or walk or move about, because the skin and muscles and organs of the body are too soft to hold themselves up. The skeleton supports the rest of the body, as the body supports the clothing we wear. Besides supporting the body, what other jobs are done by the skeleton?

1. Protecting the body. Organs such as the heart and lungs and brain are soft, and they can be easily hurt. But they are protected behind or inside hard bone. Of course, even bone will break if it is hit hard enough.

2. Helping the body to move. Muscles move every part of the body. But the muscles must be attached to something solid so they can pull against it. Suppose you wanted to drag a heavy weight across the floor. Would it be easier if you were wearing roller skates? Of course not! Wearing roller skates, you couldn't get any traction or grip on the floor when you pulled. It's the same with muscles – they need to grip onto something solid when they pull. That "something" is the skeleton.

THE BONES

The bones of the skeleton are made of cells that are as alive as any other part of the body. Aside from their role in supporting, protecting, and moving the body, bones do other jobs as well:

1. Making new cells for the blood. Blood is a liquid, but it contains millions and millions of cells. As these cells are used up, new ones are always being made inside certain bones. Bones are hard and they seem solid, but it is really only the outside of the bone that is hard. The tissue inside the bone, which is called marrow, is soft. There are small blood vessels going into the marrow and other vessels coming out. That is how blood reaches the living cells inside the bone and how new blood cells get out.

2. Storing minerals. The outside part of bone is hard because it contains a lot of minerals, mostly calcium and phosphorus. But these minerals do more than just give hardness to the bones. We always need a small amount of minerals in the blood. As the minerals in the blood start to get used up, the bones replace them by letting out some of their stored minerals. In other words, the bones are like a bank. When these minerals are needed, they come out of the bones, and when

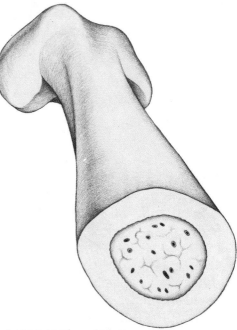

A cross-section of a bone.

there is extra mineral from the food we eat, it is deposited in the bones. If the body takes minerals out of the bones faster than the food we eat can replace them, the bones will start to soften.

Now let's look at how the bones are connected in the skeleton.

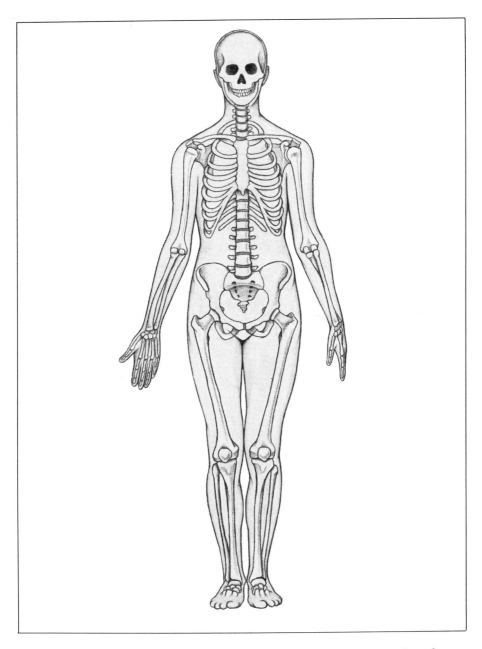

The skeleton contains 206 bones joined together. It supports and protects the soft parts of the body and anchors the muscles to allow movement.

THE JOINTS

All 206 bones in the skeleton have to be connected in some way, just as the posts and beams in the frame of a house have to be held together. In some parts of the skeleton – such as the skull and the lower part of the spine – the bones are joined so tightly that they are like a single bone. But we also need lots of connections that allow bones to move about.

A joint is a place where two or more bones come together. Wherever the body moves, bends, or twists, there are joints. The elbows are joints that let us bend or straighten our arms. The knees are joints that let us bend or straighten our legs. Now make a fist. Do you see how each finger bends in two places past the knuckle? There is a joint at each bending point, and the knuckle itself is a joint.

How can joints hold the bones together and still let them move? Think about how a door works. Hinges connect it to the door frame in the wall in such a way that the door can still swing open and closed. Hinges allow movement in only one direction. A door with hinges on one side can move back and forth, but not up and down.

Many of the joints in the body are like door hinges. But instead of metal, there are thin, strong cords called ligaments* that hold the bones together. Those ligaments, and the shapes of the bones, allow movement in only one direction. The elbows, knees, and the little joints in the fingers are hinge joints. You can bend or straighten your arms, legs, and fingers up and down, but not sideways.

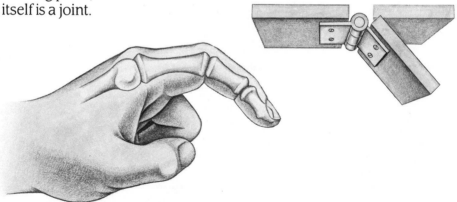

Many joints, like the fingers, are hinges. Hinge joints move only up and down.

16

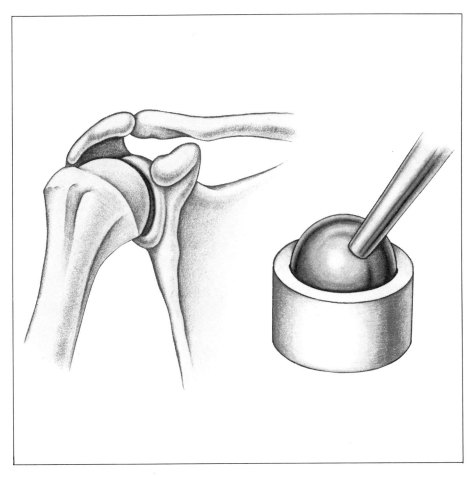

The shoulder is a ball-and-socket joint. It can move in any direction, like a joystick.

Other joints in the body let the bones move in almost any direction. Hold your arms straight at the elbows. You can raise your arms over your head or out to the sides. You can point them forward or backward. You can rotate them or swing them around in big circles. The shoulder is a ball-and-socket joint that lets the arm move in all directions. The upper end of the long bone in the upper arm is rounded, like a ball. This round end fits into a socket – an opening like a cup – at the shoulder. The hip is another ball-and-socket joint.

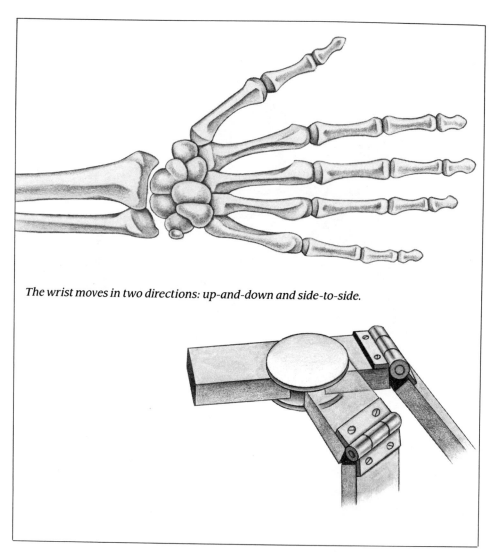

The wrist moves in two directions: up-and-down and side-to-side.

The wrist is a third type of joint. It can move up and down and from side to side, but it can't rotate. When you turn your hand palm up and then palm down, you're really turning your arm, not your wrist. Take your right arm, between the wrist and the elbow, in your left hand. Now turn your right hand palm up and then palm down. Do you feel the bones in your right arm turning? That proves that it is really your arm that is turning.

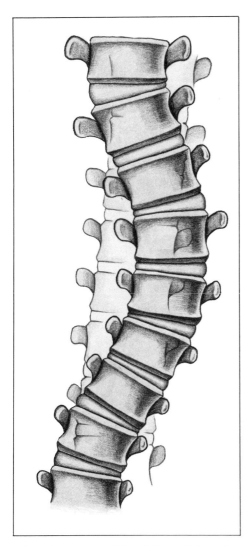

The spine turns and bends in a whole string of little joint movements.

The bones in the spine are joined in still another way, so that each joint can bend and twist a little. With so many joints so close together, the spine is very flexible. You can move your back in a whole string of little bends or twists. Notice how different that is from the way your arm moves, in one big bend at the elbow.

HOW A JOINT WORKS

A joint must allow the bones to move, but it also has to protect the bones from damage when they move.

The ends of the bones in a joint are covered by pads made of cartilage*. Cartilage is a very tough, spongy, resilient material. These pads act like rubber bumpers on a car. Just as bumpers keep a car from being dented, cartilage pads cushion the ends of the bones to keep them from crunching together when they move.

The whole joint is enclosed in a capsule. The capsule is like a sleeve. It fits closely around the bones on each side of the joint so that the space between the ends of the bones is completely sealed inside the capsule. The capsule is made of strong fibers, including the thick cords we call ligaments. These fibers hold the joint together. Muscles surround the capsule and give the joint added support.

The actual space inside the capsule, between the bones, is filled with a thick fluid called synovial fluid. Synovial means "like an egg," and this fluid has that name because it is thick, like raw egg white. Synovial fluid helps cushion the bones and lubricates the joint so the bones can glide without friction. Synovial fluid is made by the synovium*, the membrane lining the inside of the joint capsule.

Wherever muscles or tendons* have to slide over each other as the bones in the joint move, a little sac called a bursa* stays between the muscles and tendons and lets them slide smoothly. The bursa is near the joint, but outside of the capsule. *Bursitis* is inflammation of the bursa, and it can be quite painful.

WHEN A JOINT DOESN'T WORK

Every part of the joint is important for the normal working of the joint. Without the cartilage pads, the hard surfaces of the bones would crunch together. Without the capsule and the ligaments and the muscles around the capsule, the joint would come apart or the bones would move in ways that could cause great damage. Without the snyovial fluid, the joint would not move smoothly. Without the bursa, the muscles and tendons would not move easily.

In each of the different kinds of arthritis, some part of the joint is changed or damaged. The next three chapters will show what happens to the joints in the most common types of arthritis.

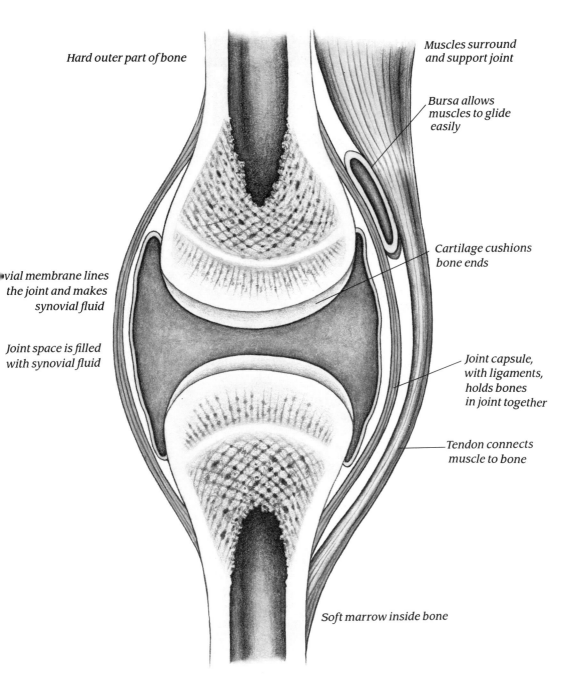

Hard outer part of bone

Muscles surround
and support joint

Bursa allows
muscles to glide
easily

vial membrane lines
the joint and makes
synovial fluid

Cartilage cushions
bone ends

Joint space is filled
with synovial fluid

Joint capsule,
with ligaments,
holds bones
in joint together

Tendon connects
muscle to bone

Soft marrow inside bone

A normal joint.

3: OSTEO-ARTHRITIS

Osteoarthritis is the most common type of arthritis, yet it does not involve much real inflammation – at least, not at first. People may have pain and stiffness, and sometimes the joints get bigger, but that is not the same thing as the swelling and heat seen in true inflammation.

The main problem in osteoarthritis is in the cartilage. The pads get worn out, and they cannot act as cushions to protect the bones from bumping together when the joint moves.

OTHER NAMES FOR OSTEOARTHRITIS

Osteo- means "bone," and *osteoarthritis* means, literally, "inflammation of the bones in a joint." But because there is very little real inflammation in this disease, and it starts in the cartilage pads rather than in the bones themselves, the name osteoarthritis doesn't describe what is happening in this disease. Some people use other names that describe the disease better.

The word *osteoarthrosis* looks very much like *osteoarthritis*, except at the end. The ending *-osis* means "a disease" or "a condition." Since this disease does not cause true inflammation, osteoarthrosis is a more accurate name, because it means simply "a condition of the bones in a joint."

Another name is degenerative joint disease. *Generate* means "make" or "build." *Degenerate* means "destroy" or "break down."

This name is useful because it tells us that the joints break down in this condition. And that is just what happens as the cartilage pads wear out.

But since osteoarthritis is the name most often used, that is what we will call the disease.

HOW CARTILAGE WORKS

If you place a sponge in a dish of water, it will absorb a lot of the water. Then if you squeeze the sponge, the water will come out. Cartilage is like a sponge – it takes in synovial fluid from inside the joint, and that fluid comes out again when the cartilage pads are squeezed between the bones moving in the joint.

As synovial fluid is slowly squeezed out of the cartilage and fills up the joint space, it keeps the bones from touching each other.

This in-and-out movement of synovial fluid also does another job. Cartilage doesn't have enough blood vessels of its own to bring in oxygen and nutrients and carry away waste products. Instead, cartilage gets what it needs from the synovial fluid that seeps in, and waste products are carried away as the fluid is pressed out of the cartilage. In other words, the synovial fluid brings oxygen and nutrients from the blood vessels to the cartilage and carries carbon dioxide and other wastes back to the blood vessels.

Can you see why movement and activity are so important? Without body movement, there wouldn't be enough in-and-out flow of fluid, and the cartilage would not stay alive and healthy.

WHEN THE PADS BECOME WORN OUT

We have to be physically active for the cartilage in our joints to be healthy. But continual activity also means that cartilage can become worn out. Healthy cartilage is tough and springy. It will come right back to its original shape when it is squeezed. However, after many years, the cartilage may become less resilient – less able to spring back after it is squeezed.

Cartilage is made up of special proteins. These proteins form strong chains that make the cartilage very tough and resilient. Eventually, after many years of use, small changes can occur that make the proteins weaker, so that the cartilage is less able to stand the pressure. That is when it starts to break down.

Most people never have any problems, because the breakdown of cartilage is too slight to notice. But some people have differences in the proteins

23

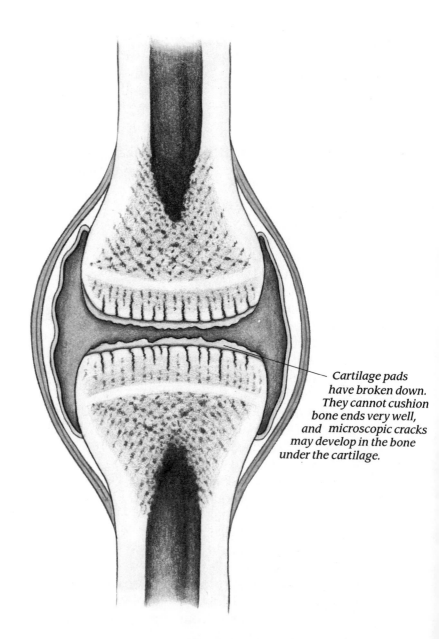

*Cartilage pads
have broken down.
They cannot cushion
bone ends very well,
and microscopic cracks
may develop in the bone
under the cartilage.*

A joint with osteoarthritis

that make up their cartilage, and these differences cause the breakdown to occur faster. Even so, osteoarthritis is very rare before the age of forty, because it usually takes much longer than that for these changes to begin.

When the cartilage pads break down, they become thinner and they can't hold as much synovial fluid as before. These changes allow the bones to come closer together. If you look at an X-ray of a joint where there is osteoarthritis, you will see that the space between the ends of the bones is smaller than normal, because the bones are closer together. The thinner and less resilient the pads become, the less they can cushion the bones moving in the joint.

As the bones start to bump harder against each other, tiny fractures (breaks) form under the cartilage. These fractures are so small that you would need a microscope to see them. They can't heal well because motion in the joint keeps forming new little fractures. This constant damage causes the ends of the bones to start forming new bone and growing outward. These changes make the whole joint wider and larger, as well as stiffer. Stiffness can also be caused by lack of use: the muscles around the joint

weaken, the ligaments contract. Unfortunately, pain makes it difficult for people to keep using and moving their joints. Cold weather can also cause stiffness, because the synovial fluid doesn't flow easily inside a cold joint.

TWO KINDS OF OSTEOARTHRITIS

The first kind of osteoarthritis (primary osteoarthritis) affects many different joints throughout the body. Joints in the fingers and the big toes, the hips and knees, and parts of the spine are often affected. The shoulders, elbows, and wrists are seldom affected in primary osteoarthritis. This is the form of osteoarthritis that we have been learning about so far, where a problem in the cartilage proteins leads to early breakdown of the cartilage.

Some cases are very mild. There may be nothing more than a knobby enlargement of the joints in the fingers. Have you ever seen a very old person with knobby finger joints? That is probably osteoarthritis. Bony knobs that form at the end-joints of the fingers have a special name: Heberden's nodes. (A node is a hard lump, and it was Dr. William Heberden who first described these growths, over two hundred years ago.) These

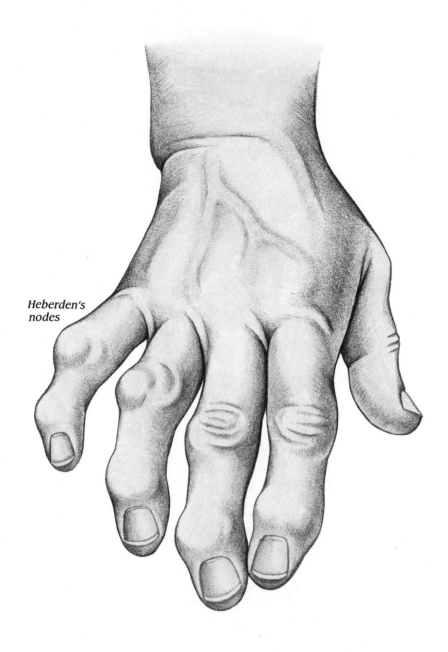

*Heberden's
nodes*

Enlarged joints from osteoarthritis are often seen in elderly people.

26

joints may be stiff, but there is not much pain.

In the joints of the spine, an extra pad called a disk keeps the bones separated and well cushioned. When the joints in the spine are affected by arthritis, these disks break down, not the cartilage itself. Again, the main problem may be stiffness. But if the spaces between the bones in the spine become narrow, the bones may start pressing on nerves, and that can be painful.

Osteoarthritis in the hips and knees is very painful, because these joints have to support the weight of the body and that pressure causes pain in the diseased joints.

In the other type of osteoarthritis (secondary osteoarthritis), the breakdown of cartilage happens because of some special problem in the area. An injury to the joint may cause secondary osteoarthritis years later. An infection in the joint may be the cause. Or it may be a poor supply of blood to the joint. Even something as simple as being overweight places too much stress on the cartilage in the hips and knees.

Secondary osteoarthritis can happen wherever there has been a problem in a joint. It does not always affect the same joints that are usually affected in primary osteoarthritis.

At one time, doctors thought that all osteoarthritis was a simple matter of "wear-and-tear" that would affect anyone, sooner or later. But they noticed that people who do hard physical work are actually less likely to get arthritis than people who are inactive. Now we know that it is the people with abnormal cartilage proteins who get primary osteoarthritis, even from normal activities, while it takes injury or special stresses to produce secondary osteoarthritis, and that can happen in anyone.

WHAT HAPPENS TO THE PATIENT?

Osteoarthritis can affect one joint or many joints, and it can be very mild or severe. But there are certain features of the disease that are common.

First, there is pain, as the cartilage wears out and lets the bones bump against each other. The more the joint is used, the worse the pain will be. The pain is usually worse at the end of the day's activity. Rest relieves the pain, so there is usually less pain in the morning, after a night's sleep.

Stiffness is the opposite: It is worse after rest and relieved by activity. If a joint stops moving, it is serving no purpose, so the goal is to fight stiffness with activity, even though it hurts.

New bone formation at the edges of the joint can cause permanent stiffness of the joint. However, once the joint becomes "frozen" (unable to move), there may be less pain.

The damage to the bones can cause real inflammation inside the joint. When this happens, the name osteoarthritis is accurate, even though the disease did not start out with inflammation.

In most cases, treatment of osteoarthritis is very helpful. In Chapter Seven, we'll see how the disease is treated.

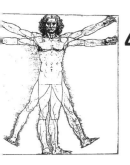

4: RHEUMATOID ARTHRITIS

In Chapter One, we said that the word *rheumatism* doesn't have any exact meaning. But the word *rheumatoid* in the disease called rheumatoid arthritis is different. It comes from the same root as rheumatism: *rheum*, an old word that describes stiffness, fatigue, and aching in the body. The ending *-oid* means "similar to." Rheumatoid arthritis is a form of arthritis that is similar to rheum, because patients with this form of arthritis are often tired and they suffer from stiffness in the joints and aching in the body.

As many as six million Americans have rheumatoid arthritis, and there are about 80 thousand new cases every year in this country. Three out of four patients are women. The disease usually appears when someone is about thirty-five to forty-five years old, but it could start at any time from childhood to old age.

This arthritis is a synovitis, an inflammation of the synovium, the membrane that lines the inside of the joint capsule.

INFLAMMATION

We saw earlier how inflammation happens. When the body's tissues are damaged, certain types of white blood cells travel to that area to repair the damage. As they work, fluid builds up and there is greater blood flow in the damaged area. The result is inflammation: a combination of swelling, warmth, redness, and pain. Normally, these signs of inflammation show that white blood cells are doing their job. When the damage has been repaired, the inflammation goes away.

A healthy synovium is thin. It folds and bends easily, and it makes a thick synovial fluid to cushion and lubricate the joint. But in rheumatoid arthritis, inflammation of the synovium only leads to more inflammation. When the membrane becomes inflamed, more and more white blood cells enter it and it starts growing until it is thick and swollen. The inflammation itself causes more damage, and that causes more inflammation.

No one knows what starts all this inflammation. Many doctors think it is some kind of microscopic organism. Whatever it is, it doesn't affect most people. But people who get rheumatoid arthritis are probably born with a defect in their immune system*, the body's defense system. They cannot fight off the organism, and a harmful inflammation is the result.

We can tell that there is a problem in the immune system because most people with rheumatoid arthritis have "rheumatoid factor" in the blood. One of the ways the immune system works is by building special proteins called antibodies*. Normally, antibodies work against harmful bacteria or anything else that doesn't belong in the body. Rheumatoid factor is an abnormal antibody that works against other parts of the immune system. Its presence in the blood is a marker that helps confirm the diagnosis of rheumatoid arthritis (see Chapter Six).

WHAT HAPPENS IN RHEUMATOID ARTHRITIS?

In a person with rheumatoid arthritis, the damaged synovium pours a large amount of synovial fluid into the joint space. Swelling in rheumatoid arthritis is caused by two things: the thickened synovium and the large amount of synovial fluid. But the fluid made by the damaged synovium is thinner than normal synovial fluid. It can't lubricate the joint and cushion the bones very well.

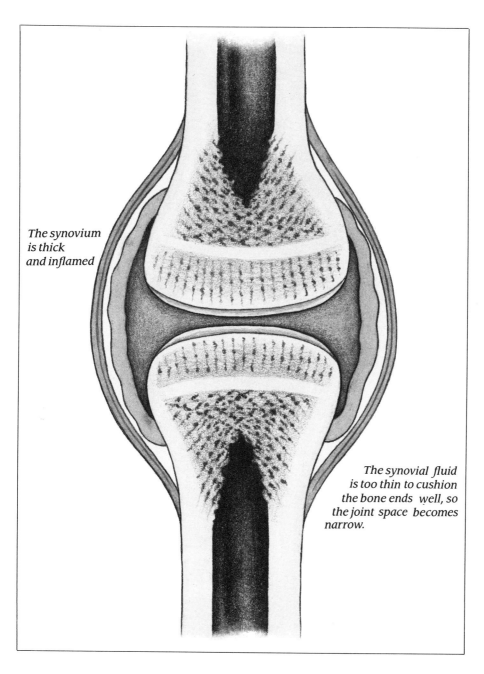

The synovium is thick and inflamed

The synovial fluid is too thin to cushion the bone ends well, so the joint space becomes narrow.

A joint with rheumatoid arthritis

The bones start bumping and rubbing against each other. The cartilage begins to break down. The joint space between the bones gets smaller, and the ends of the bones wear away. Even the ligaments are damaged, and that causes the bones in the joint to slip out of position.

Rheumatoid arthritis affects many joints, on both sides of the body at the same time. Joints in the hands and wrists are very often affected. So are the shoulders, hips, knees, and joints in the feet. Pain and stiffness are worst in the morning. Activity helps to relieve the stiffness.

But rheumatoid arthritis is more than just a joint disease. It can affect many different parts of the body: the eye, the skin, the blood vessels, the heart, the lungs, the muscles, and the nervous system. Many patients with this disease feel tired and achy all the time.

Some people have very bad cases of rheumatoid arthritis, and in other people the disease can be kept under control. Treatment is aimed at fighting inflammation (see Chapter Seven).

JUVENILE RHEUMATOID ARTHRITIS

Children can sometimes get the same kind of rheumatoid arthritis that adults get. But the disease called juvenile rheumatoid arthritis is a different disease. It is also called Still's disease, named after Frederic Still, who was the first person to describe it.

In very young children, boys and girls are affected in equal numbers. When it starts in older children, girls are more often affected.

There is no marker in the blood, in many cases. Some forms of this disease are similar to adult-type rheumatoid arthritis, and rheumatoid factor is found in a number of those cases.

Some cases cause a lot of permanent damage to the joints, and others can be treated to prevent damage. The treatment is like the treatment for adult-type rheumatoid arthritis, except that the doses of drugs are smaller for children.

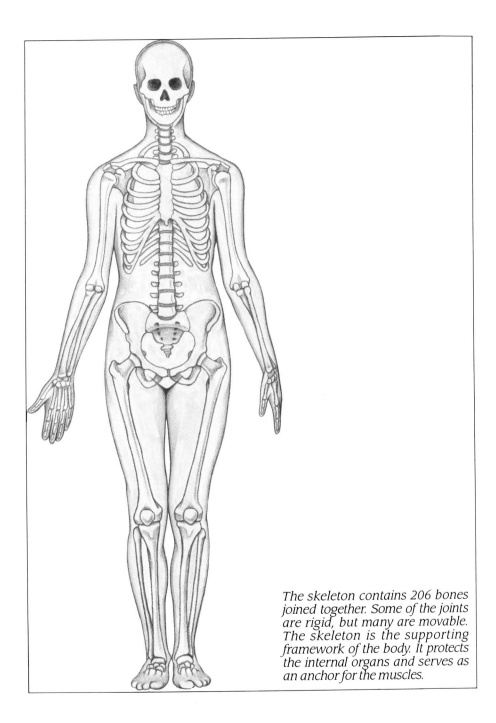

The skeleton contains 206 bones joined together. Some of the joints are rigid, but many are movable. The skeleton is the supporting framework of the body. It protects the internal organs and serves as an anchor for the muscles.

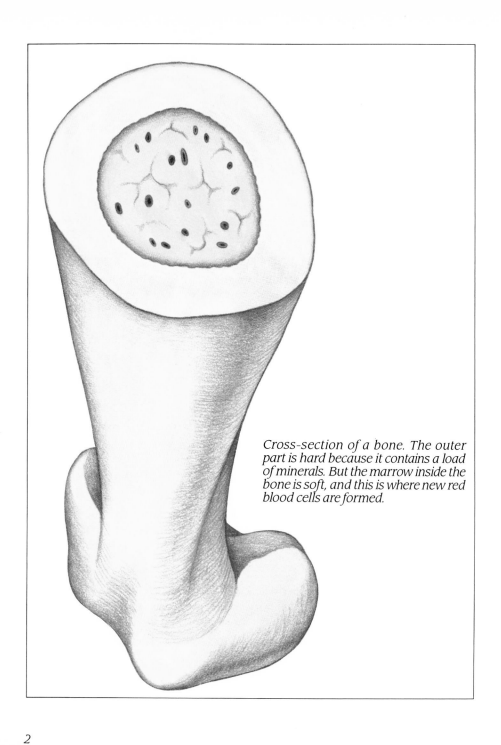

Cross-section of a bone. The outer part is hard because it contains a load of minerals. But the marrow inside the bone is soft, and this is where new red blood cells are formed.

Many joints, like those in the fingers, are hinges. Hinge joints work like the hinges on a door, allowing movement in only one direction (up and down).

The shoulder is a ball-and-socket joint. It can move in any direction, like a joystick. That is why the arms can move forward, backward, outward, upward, or in big circles. The hip is another ball-and-socket joint.

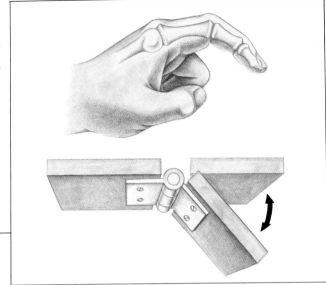

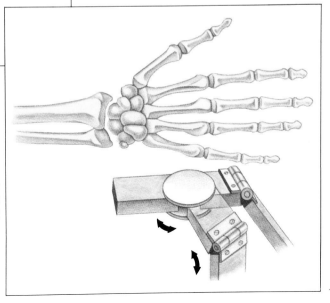

The wrist moves in two directions: up and down, and side to side. But it cannot rotate. When the hand is turned over, it is the forearm that rotates, not the wrist.

3

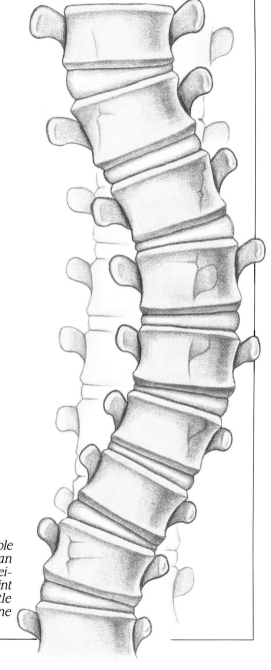

The spine turns and bends in a whole string of little joint movements. It can bend forward or backward or to either side, and it can rotate. Each joint moves only a little, but all the little movements together make the spine flexible.

Bursa

tilage

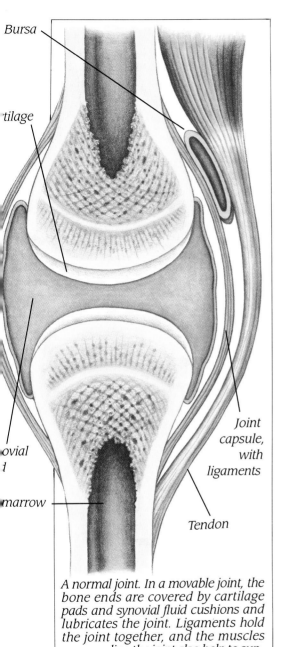

ovial
i

marrow

Joint
capsule,
with
ligaments

Tendon

A normal joint. In a movable joint, the bone ends are covered by cartilage pads and synovial fluid cushions and lubricates the joint. Ligaments hold the joint together, and the muscles surrounding the joint also help to support it.

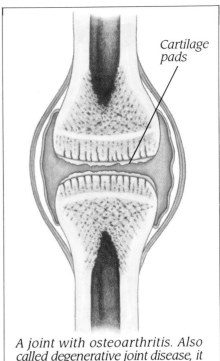

Cartilage
pads

A joint with osteoarthritis. Also called degenerative joint disease, it is the most common type of arthritis. Yet there is little true inflammation involved in this condition.

Enlarged joints from osteoarthritis are often seen in elderly people. Heberden's nodes are found near the ends of the fingers.

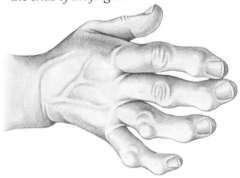

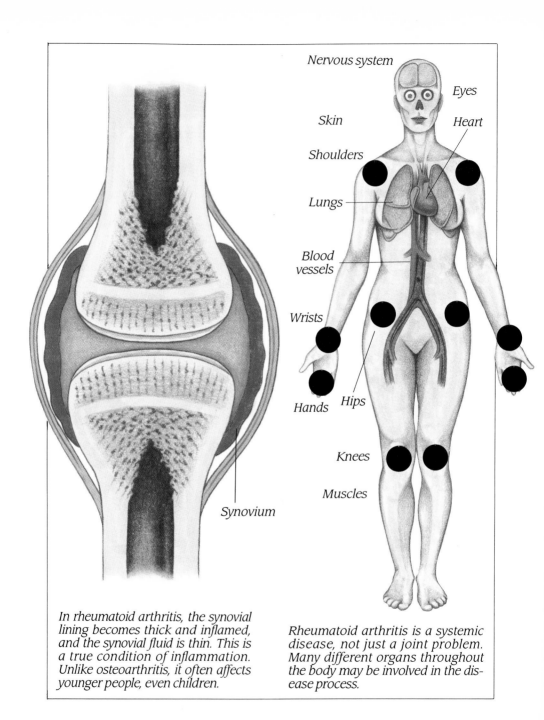

Nervous system

Eyes

Skin

Heart

Shoulders

Lungs

Blood vessels

Wrists

Hands   Hips

Knees

Muscles

Synovium

In rheumatoid arthritis, the synovial lining becomes thick and inflamed, and the synovial fluid is thin. This is a true condition of inflammation. Unlike osteoarthritis, it often affects younger people, even children.

Rheumatoid arthritis is a systemic disease, not just a joint problem. Many different organs throughout the body may be involved in the disease process.

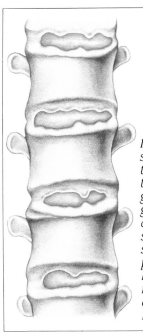

In ankylosing spondylitis, the bones of the spine start growing together. This disease is sometimes seen in young people who have inflammatory disease of the intestines.

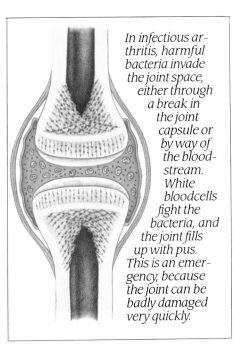

In infectious arthritis, harmful bacteria invade the joint space, either through a break in the joint capsule or by way of the blood-stream. White bloodcells fight the bacteria, and the joint fills up with pus. This is an emergency, because the joint can be badly damaged very quickly.

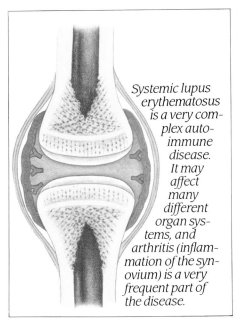

Systemic lupus erythematosus is a very complex auto-immune disease. It may affect many different organ systems, and arthritis (inflammation of the synovium) is a very frequent part of the disease.

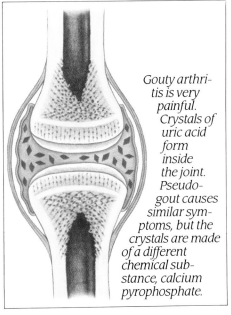

Gouty arthritis is very painful. Crystals of uric acid form inside the joint. Pseudo-gout causes similar symptoms, but the crystals are made of a different chemical substance, calcium pyrophosphate.

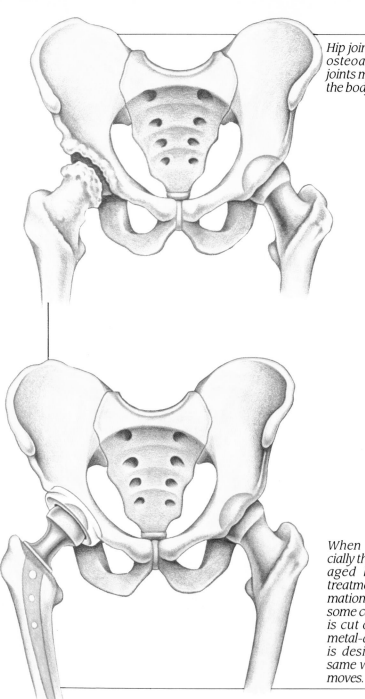

Hip joints are often affected by osteoarthritis, since these joints must support so much of the body's weight.

When certain joints – especially the hips – are badly damaged by arthritis, medical treatment for pain and inflammation may not be enough. In some cases, the damaged joint is cut out and replaced by a metal-and-plastic device that is designed to move in the same way as the normal joint moves.

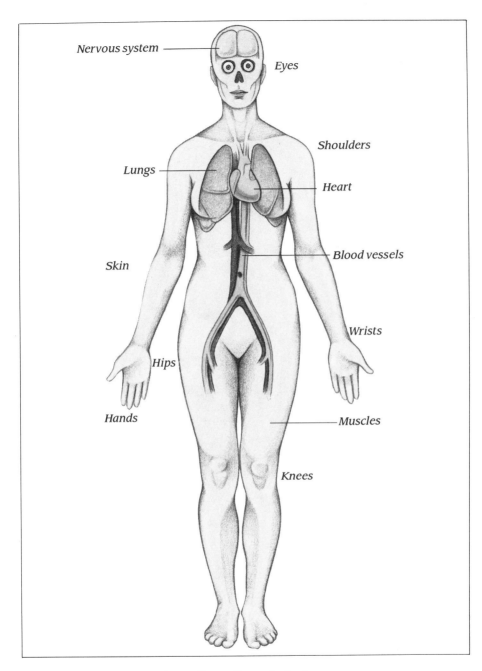

Rheumatoid arthritis may have effects all over the body.

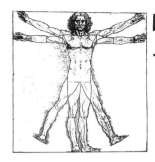

5: OTHER KINDS OF ARTHRITIS

We have just looked at the two most common forms of arthritis, osteoarthritis and rheumatoid arthritis. Now we'll learn about some other kinds of arthritis.

INFECTIOUS ARTHRITIS

If bacteria* ("germs") get into a joint, they can grow very fast and the whole joint can fill up with pus, a thick, bad-smelling liquid full of bacteria. An infected joint is a medical emergency. The large joints, especially the knees, are the ones most likely to get infected.

If the joint is sealed up inside a capsule, how can bacteria get inside? There are two ways that can happen.

1. The joint capsule could be broken open – ripped or punctured by accident, or cut open during an operation. Staphylococcus* is the organism that most often causes infection when the joint capsule is opened. Anyone can get this kind of joint infection.

2. Bacteria in the blood can reach the joint through the vessels that go to the synovial membrane lining the capsule. As the membrane makes synovial fluid, the bacteria enter the joint. In children, a germ called Hemophilus* is the most common cause of joint infection that comes from the bloodstream. But in adults, it is a germ called

34

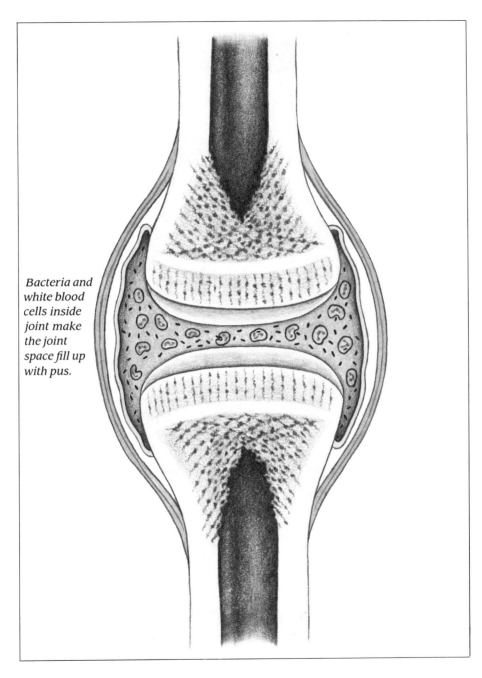

Bacteria and white blood cells inside joint make the joint space fill up with pus.

Infectious arthritis

gonococcus*, and joint infection from gonococcus in the blood occurs most often in young women. Gonorrhea, a disease caused by gonococcus, is spread by sexual contact. In men, it causes so much discomfort that they get it treated right away, before the bacteria can enter the blood. But gonorrhea doesn't cause as much discomfort in women; they may not even know they have the disease. Meanwhile, the bacteria have time to spread through the bloodstream, eventually reaching the joints.

If infectious arthritis is attended to quickly (see Chapter Seven), treatment is usually successful. If the infection is not treated in time, the whole joint could be destroyed.

GOUT AND PSEUDOGOUT

In gout*, crystals of a chemical called uric acid form inside the joints, causing intense inflammation. Uric acid is a normal part of blood, but some people have much more than the normal amount. There is a limit to how much of any substance can be dissolved in a liquid. (You can dissolve only a certain amount of sugar in a glass of water. Once the water is saturated with sugar, any more sugar you add will just settle to the bottom of the glass, no matter how much you stir it.) Any uric acid more than the blood can hold will form crystals in many parts of the body, including the joints.

The joint involved is most often in the big toe. The toe becomes warm, red, and swollen with inflammation, which causes terrible pain. Gout may also strike other joints, but that happens less often.

The body may be able to absorb these crystals, and the problem may go away. But gout often comes back, again and again. After many years, uric acid starts forming tophi* (hard chunks) in other parts of the body, especially the ears and the skin near the joints.

Pseudogout means "false gout." It is also caused by crystals, but they are made of a mineral called calcium pyrophosphate. These crystals can form inside cartilage as people get older, and can then enter the joint space, again causing great pain.

Doctors can look at the crystals under a special light to see whether they are uric acid or calcium pyrophosphate. That's important to know, because the treatment for the conditions are different (see Chapter Seven).

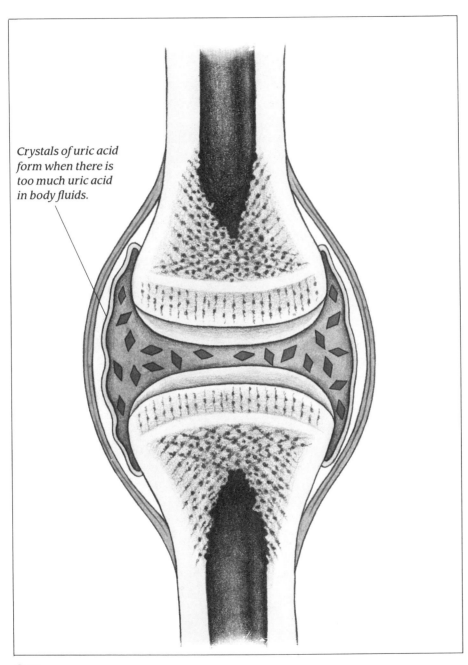

Crystals of uric acid form when there is too much uric acid in body fluids.

Gout

ANKYLOSING SPONDYLITIS

*Ankylosing** means "stiffening of a joint." *Spondylitis* means "arthritis of the spine." This form of arthritis makes the joints in the spine stiff.

It is a type of genetic disease. Ankylosing spondylitis is much more common in people who have a gene called Human Leukocyte Antigen B27 (B27) than in people who don't have it.

The disease starts in the lower part of the back. The joints here do not have a synovial lining – only fibers and ligaments that hold the joint together. These joints don't have very much range of movement. Inflammation begins where the ligaments are attached to the bones, causing pain when there is any movement. After a while, the bones start growing together until they are fused (connected into one piece). Then there is no movement at all.

Even so, it is usually a mild disease. Many kinds of arthritis are more common in women, but men are more likely to have problems from ankylosing spondylitis. Most people learn to live with stiffness in the spine, but sometimes the disease spreads up the back. In bad cases, patients may end up with the whole spine fused, so they can't move their heads or turn their bodies at all. The best thing patients can do is stretching exercises to fight stiffness and to keep the bones from becoming fused.

REITER'S SYNDROME

A German doctor named Hans Reiter was the first person to study this condition, during World War I. It happens most often in young men. There are three problems that go together in this syndrome*: arthritis, an inflammation inside the eye, and an inflammation inside the penis. The arthritis most often affects the spine, the heels, or the toes.

Reiter's syndrome is another disease that appears most often in people who have the B27 gene. It is believed to be triggered by a bacterial infection. If these people get that kind of infection, the B27 gene makes them more likely to develop this syndrome.

In most cases, Reiter's syndrome occurs after sexual contact, but it can also come from an infection in the intestines. Even though it is related to the presence of bacteria, doctors aren't sure whether treatment with antibiotic drugs is helpful. The main treatment for Reiter's syndrome is anti-inflammatory drugs (see Chapter Seven).

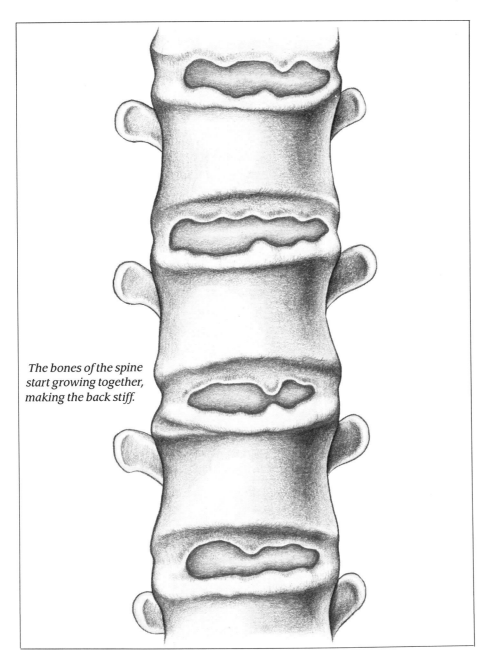

The bones of the spine start growing together, making the back stiff.

Ankylosing spondylitis

LUPUS

The full name of this complex disease is systemic lupus* erythematosus. Systemic means that it affects the whole body. *Lupus* means "wolf" – some patients get a rash that makes their skin look eroded (as if chewed by a wild animal). Erythematosus just means that this rash is red.

Lupus occurs most often in young women. It involves the body's immune system. In Chapter Four, we learned a little about how the immune system makes antibodies that work against things that don't belong in the body. People with lupus have a defect in the immune system: it doesn't recognize the body's tissues as its own, and it treats those tissues as if they didn't belong in the body. The immune system then makes antibodies that work against the body's own tissues. These antibodies can cause great damage. This is called autoimmunity ("immunity against self").

One of these abnormal antibodies is called antinuclear antibody. It is found in most people with lupus, which helps to identify the disease (see Chapter Six).

In lupus, the damage affects many parts of the body, including the joints. Arthritis is a common feature, but that is only one part of the disease. The arthritis in lupus is like rheumatoid arthritis: a synovial inflammation.

Apart from arthritis, lupus can also cause problems in the linings around the heart and lungs, or in the skin or nervous system. But the worst harm comes when the kidneys are affected – this development can be fatal. In most cases, however, lupus is not that bad, and it can usually be treated very well (see Chapter Seven).

PSORIATIC ARTHRITIS

Psoriasis* is a common skin condition. It causes red, flaky patches on the skin, usually at the knees and elbows. A few people who have psoriasis also have arthritis. Sometimes, the skin disease and the joint disease have nothing to do with each other. But in certain cases, the two conditions go together, and this is called psoriatic arthritis.

The arthritis is similar to rheumatoid arthritis. Most of the time, it is a mild condition. But it can also be more serious. In a few cases, it can cripple the patient.

Treatment is usually like the treatment for rheumatoid arthritis. Bad cases call for drugs that suppress the body's immune system (see Chapter Seven).

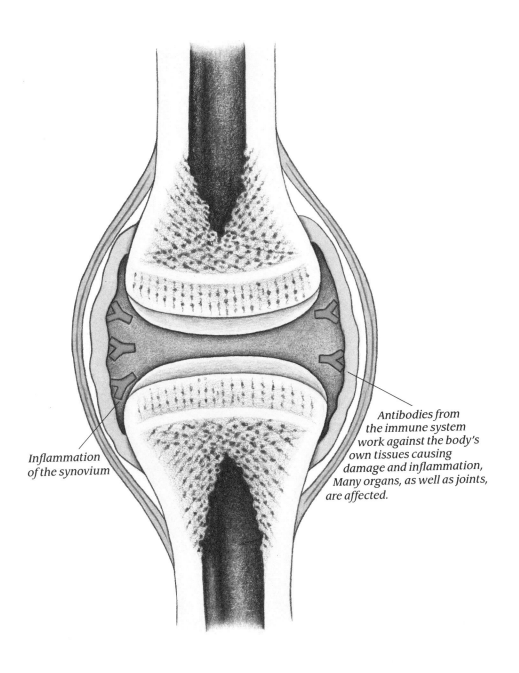

Inflammation
of the synovium

Antibodies from
the immune system
work against the body's
own tissues causing
damage and inflammation,
Many organs, as well as joints,
are affected.

Lupus

41

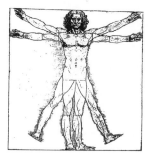

6: FINDING OUT WHO HAS ARTHRITIS

Suppose a person sees a doctor because of pain in the bones and joints. Is it arthritis or something else? And if it is arthritis, what form of the disease is it?

Doctors figure out what is wrong with a sick person in three ways: asking questions, examining the patient, and doing tests.

THE HISTORY

The first step in a doctor's evaluation is called "taking a history." What the patient feels are called "symptoms." The doctor will ask many questions about symptoms and about the person who has the problem. If the problem is pain in the joints, the doctor will ask where the pain is located, which joints are involved, when it started, whether it is worse in the morning or in the evening, whether there is stiffness as well as pain, and whether there are any other problems besides the pain.

All this information helps the doctor see what the problem could be. For example, a young woman who wakes up every morning with pain and stiffness in both wrists and hands could have rheumatoid arthritis. But an old man with pain in the hip, which gets worse during the day, is more likely to have osteoarthritis. And a young man with severe inflammation in one knee, as well as pain when urinating and discomfort in the eye, probably has Reiter's syndrome.

The doctor won't know for sure what the problem is just from taking a history. The next step is the physical examination, and that will either confirm what the doctor suspects from the history, or it will point to something else.

THE PHYSICAL EXAMINATION

In each painful area, the doctor will feel the joints and muscles. Does the joint feel warm and swollen? Or knobby and hard? Can the joint move smoothly, or does it seem to be scraping as it moves? Are the muscles sore around the joint? Or do they look shrunken and weak? Is the joint moving in its normal direction, or does it seem to be twisted?

The doctor will also examine the rest of the patient's body to see if there is anything else unusual, such as fever, a rash on the skin, or nodules (small hard lumps under the skin). What the doctor finds during the physical examination are called "signs." Warmth and soft swelling in the joints are more likely to be seen in someone with rheumatoid arthritis than in someone with osteoarthritis.

In many cases, the diagnosis will be clear from the history and physical examination. But just to be sure, the doctor will order tests to confirm the diagnosis and tell how serious the disease is.

DIAGNOSTIC TESTS

X-rays are electromagnetic rays that can go right through certain objects. They can go through the muscles and organs and other soft parts of the body, but not through solid bone. When the rays go all the way through, they hit a photographic film. Wherever the rays are stopped by something hard and solid (like bones, teeth, or metal fillings in teeth), the film is not exposed. That shows the shape and position of the solid parts.

The doctor will take X-rays of the painful joints to see if there is any injury in the bone. Or if the joint space between the ends of the bones is smaller than normal. Or if the bones are growing in new shapes or are pointing in strange directions. Or if the bones are losing some of their minerals. Or if the bone edges look worn away.

Another kind of test is to examine the blood for markers. In

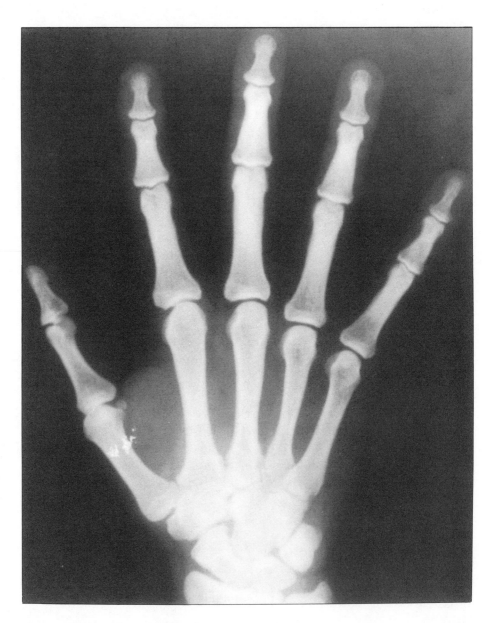

An x-ray picture of a normal hand.

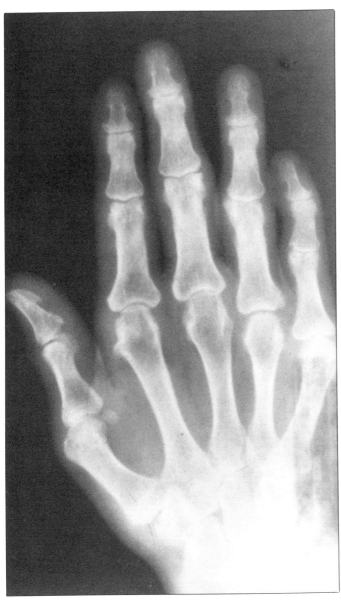

An x-ray picture of a hand with rheumatoid arthritis. The dark bones have lost some minerals. Notice how the fifth finger's middle joint has slipped, allowing the finger to bend backward.

certain kinds of arthritis, there are markers that act like name tags for the disease, and most patients with these diseases have these markers. Most adult patients with rheumatoid arthritis have rheumatoid factor. Antinuclear antibody is the marker for lupus.

Usually, the more of the marker there is in the patient's blood, the more active the disease is. If the history and physical examination point to one of the diseases that have markers, the doctor will try to confirm the diagnosis by testing for the marker for the suspected disease.

However, many kinds of arthritis don't produce any markers. Some patients with rheumatoid arthritis do not have rheumatoid factor at all. And some people have the marker although they do not have the disease. That is one reason these tests cannot take the place of the history and physical examination. Another reason is that no laboratory test is perfect.

Another helpful test is looking at the synovial fluid. The doctor puts a needle right into the joint and takes out some of the fluid. Sometimes this will tell what is causing the arthritis. For example, if the fluid has harmful bacteria in it, the problem is infection. If the fluid contains crystals, the diagnosis is gout or pseudogout. But if there is no infection and no crystals, testing the fluid can tell only whether or not there is inflammation.

A biopsy* is removal of a bit of tissue from the patient's body for close examination. It might be a bit of skin or muscle, or a tiny piece taken from a blood vessel or a kidney or from the synovial lining of the joint capsule. Doctors called pathologists look at such bits of tissue under a microscope to find out what kind of disease is present.

OTHER LABORATORY TESTS

In many diseases with long-lasting inflammation, production of red blood cells goes down. Having too few red blood cells is a condition called anemia.* Anemia can also be caused by bleeding, and some of the medicines used to treat arthritis can cause the stomach and intestines to bleed slowly. Patients with arthritis can have anemia from both of those causes. The complete blood count measures several things, including the number of red blood cells, to tell the doctor if the patient has anemia.

The same test will also show how many white blood cells the

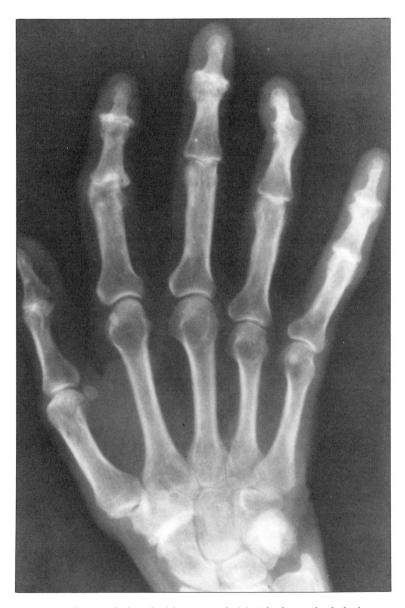

An x-ray picture of a hand with osteoarthritis. The bones look darker because they have lost some of their minerals. See how the space is gone in the joints at the ends of the fingers.

patient has. A small number of people who have very bad cases of rheumatoid arthritis have to take powerful drugs, and these drugs can damage the white blood cells of the body.

A very simple and useful test is called the sedimentation rate. The word *sediment* means something solid that settles to the bottom of a liquid (like silt settling to the bottom of a lake). If a thin tube of blood is left standing, the red blood cells will separate from the plasma (the liquid part of blood) and settle to the bottom of the tube. The sedimentation rate shows how fast the blood cells fall. When there is inflammation, the rate is faster than when there is no inflammation. This test can show whether or not there is any inflammation, and whether treatment is making the inflammation go away.

Urine tests are done to see if the patient's kidneys are working properly. Lupus can affect the kidneys, and some of the drugs used to treat bad cases of arthritis can damage the kidneys. So it is important to watch the condition of the patient's kidneys in these situations.

TREATMENT DEPENDS ON THE DIAGNOSIS

X-rays and blood tests are done in almost all cases, because they are safe and easy to perform. Tests like biopsy or taking a sample of synovial fluid are done only when there is a definite reason to do them, because the tests themselves can be painful.

The combined information – from the history, the physical examination, and tests – helps the doctor make a diagnosis and keep watch on the patient's general health. Then treatment can begin. In the next chapter, we'll look at the treatment of arthritis.

7: TREATING ARTHRITIS

There is no cure for arthritis. Doctors can help patients live with arthritis, but they can't make the disease go away.

Then what does treatment do, if it doesn't cure the disease? Treatment can (1) relieve pain, (2) keep joints working as long as possible, (3) stop the disease from getting worse, or at least slow down its progress.

These three goals are related to each other. For example, relieving pain allows the patient to do the kinds of exercise that keep the joint working. Inflammation causes pain; it also causes damage to the joint. Therefore, drugs that fight inflammation also relieve pain and slow down the damage being done.

DRUGS TO FIGHT PAIN AND INFLAMMATION

Aspirin is the drug most commonly used for arthritis. Treatment of most types of arthritis begins with aspirin. Aspirin works against prostaglandins – those complex substances formed when cells are damaged and which trigger pain in the area of damage. At low doses, aspirin simply fights pain. At much higher doses, it fights inflammation. To relieve a lot of inflammation, very high doses of aspirin are needed. But at those doses, aspirin can have serious side effects: a ringing noise in the ears and bleeding inside the stomach and intestines.

Instead of giving such high doses of aspirin, most doctors would rather use other drugs that work the same way. These are called nonsteroidal anti-inflammatory drugs. (This is a long name, but it is easy to understand: Anti-inflammatory means that these drugs fight inflammation, and nonsteroidal means that they are not corticosteroids,* which are a very different kind of anti-inflammatory drug. Doctors call these nonsteroidal anti-inflammatory drugs by the initials NSAID.)

NSAIDs also block prostaglandins to fight inflammation, and they produce fewer side effects than high doses of aspirin. But they are more expensive than aspirin. In most cases, doctors will try aspirin first, and then change to NSAIDs if there is a lot of inflammation or if the patient is having bad side effects from aspirin.

There are other drugs that are very good at fighting inflammation, but they can have serious side effects and they are used less often. These drugs are corticosteroids, gold salts, penicillamine (not the common antibiotic penicillin), and chloroquine (a drug used to treat the tropical disease malaria and found to be a good drug for reducing inflammation in arthritis).

SPECIAL TREATMENTS

Fighting pain and inflammation is always important, but there are two kinds of arthritis that require special treatment.

In infectious arthritis, the doctor tests some synovial fluid taken out of the joint with a needle. Once the germ that is causing the infection is found, the right antibiotic* drug is given. In some cases, the doctor has to try to drain out the infected fluid from the joint with a needle. If that doesn't work, the patient may need a surgical operation to open up the joint and clean out the infection.

In gout, the patient has too much uric acid, which forms crystals in the joint. NSAIDs are good for fighting the pain and inflammation, but the doctor must also use a drug that will help the patient get rid of uric acid. Those drugs won't help in pseudogout, because the crystals in that condition are not made of uric acid.

DRUGS THAT WORK ON THE IMMUNE SYSTEM

Some of the drugs used to treat cancer are effective in certain kinds of arthritis. Arthritis is not a form of cancer, but doctors believe that both diseases have something to do with the body's immune system (see Chapter Four). Many drugs that are used against cancer work on the immune system, and certain kinds of arthritis, such as rheumatoid arthritis, are definitely related to the immune system. Drugs like cyclophosphamide and methotrexate can sometimes stop arthritis from spreading and doing more damage. They are also used in bad cases of Reiter's syndrome and psoriatic arthritis.

The trouble is that these drugs are dangerous – so dangerous that they aren't used at all unless the disease is damaging the whole body, not just the joints.

SURGERY FOR ARTHRITIS

Sometimes a patient will still have a lot of pain, or joint destruction will still be getting worse, despite full treatment with drugs. In such cases, an operation may be necessary. There are several kinds of surgery that are done for arthritis.

If a joint has become badly damaged, it can be cut out and replaced with a mechanical joint made of metal and plastic. This operation is done most often on the hip joint, and it usually works very well. Joint replacement has also been done on the knee and ankle and the small joints in the fingers.

A fusion operation connects two bones so tightly that they become like one bone. Of course, the joint can't move at all after that. But fusion can be helpful if a joint has become weak and unstable (unable to hold the bones in the right position). Fusion is done most often at the ankle or wrist. It might be difficult to walk if your ankle doesn't bend, but it's better than trying to walk with an ankle that can't hold you up.

If the synovial lining of a joint has become thick from inflammation, it sometimes helps to remove it. Removal of the synovial lining reduces inflammation and damage inside the joint.

WHAT PATIENTS CAN DO

What patients do for themselves can be just as important as drugs and surgery for arthritis.

First, patients should try to stay in good health. That means being careful to avoid accidents and infections, not smoking, and

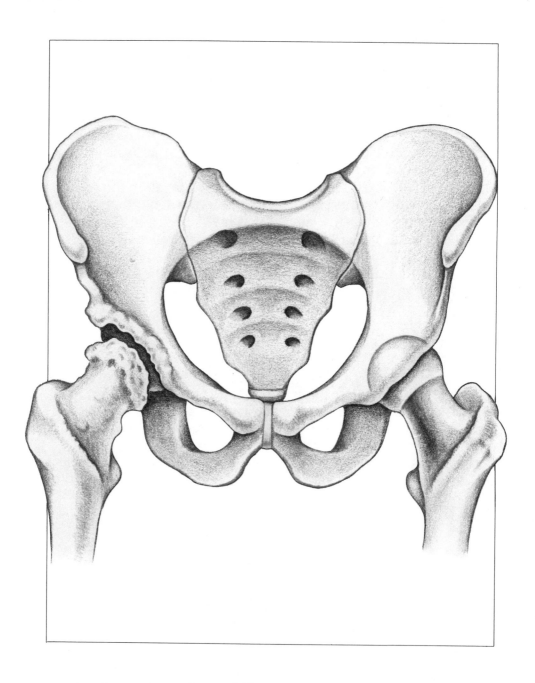

Hip joints showing damage from arthritis.

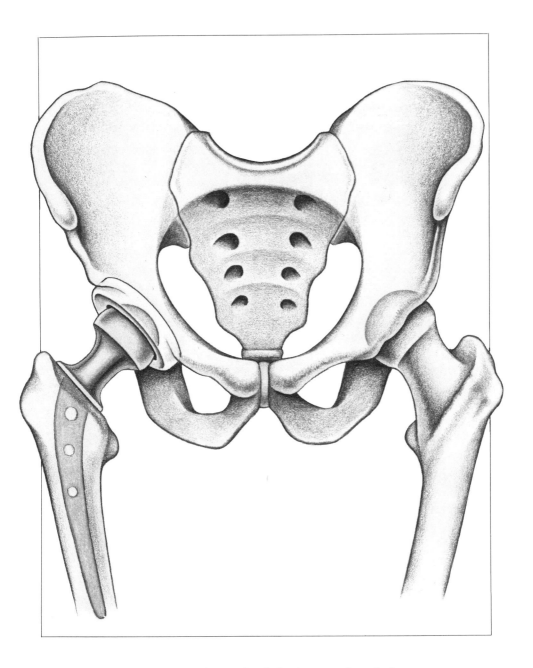

Joint replacement surgery puts in metal and plastic parts where the bones were badly damaged.

following a good, balanced diet.

Second, people with arthritis should not be overweight. Extra weight places extra strain on joints like the hips and knees, which can make arthritis in those joints much worse. A patient who is overweight must try to reduce – not by starving or by any strange diet, but just by eating sensibly. Being the correct weight is important for general health as well as for dealing with arthritis.

Third, exercise and physical activity are very important for keeping the joints working. Without exercise, the muscles will shrink and weaken, and the joints can become unstable. Supplying the cartilage with oxygen and nutrition depends on moving the joint. The bones themselves will lose minerals and become soft and weak if they don't move. You can see why exercise is so important.

Exercise can make inflammation worse, but only for a little while. Most doctors agree that exercise is necessary even when there is inflammation. In fact, some doctors think that the main job done by anti-inflammatory drugs is to allow the patient to exercise more.

A good exercise program starts slowly and builds up. Stretching exercises fight stiffness and keep the joints moving. That is very important in a condition such as ankylosing spondylitis, in which stiffness is the main problem. Exercises also keep the muscles strong. The best exercises move the joints back and forth, again and again, without strain. Walking and swimming are very good exercises.

Rest is also important. Resting a joint reduces inflammation. Patients with rheumatoid arthritis often feel so tired and stiff that they may want to rest all the time instead of exercising. But they need both – rest as well as exercise. The doctor can help plan how much rest and exercise each patient needs.

FAKE CURES

Some patients who have suffered from arthritis for a long time look for cures outside of medical treatment. People who sell fake medical cures are called "quacks" – and you might as well listen to a duck quacking as follow the advice of people who sell fake cures for arthritis!

Apart from wasting money, the person with arthritis can be hurt by fake cures. Some of these cures are actually dangerous.

One of the oldest fake cures is a copper bracelet worn around the wrist. It is harmless – and also worthless.

Books that describe special diets to cure arthritis are another kind of fake. No diet can cure the disease. A sensible, balanced diet is good for general health and for getting rid of extra weight, but that is all.

Pills and injections that are supposed to cure arthritis are worse than worthless – they are dangerous. Most of these medicines contain corticosteroids. Remember, corticosteroids are very powerful anti-inflammatory drugs, but they have a lot of side effects. These drugs do relieve symptoms, but only for a little while, so the person will have to keep taking the drug. The longer it is taken, the worse the side effects. That's why doctors don't give corticosteroids to everyone with arthritis.

Some quacks tell people to stop taking regular medical treatment, and some people have followed that advice – and their arthritis got much worse.

It is easy to spot a fake cure: Anything that promises to cure arthritis is a fake. If you read or hear about a new treatment and you want to know whether it is worthwhile, ask your doctor about it.

8: RESEARCH IN ARTHRITIS

Some people look for miracles from quacks who sell fake cures. Other people look for miracles from medical research.

There is a lot of research in arthritis, but it probably won't lead to any miracle cures. Researchers are always looking for safer and more effective drugs and better ways to do operations for arthritis. For example, there is research going on to develop mechanical joints for replacement of the shoulder and other new areas. But these are not cures.

Research on the immune system may teach us more about the causes and prevention of arthritis. The most important thing that doctors have learned is

that some kinds of arthritis can be avoided. For example, by avoiding accidents and injuries, by exercising properly and not being overweight, people can reduce their risk of getting arthritis. And if they do get any kind of arthritis, it probably won't be as bad as in someone who is overweight and gets no exercise.

The person who gets arthritis does not have to wait and hope for miracles. Yes, treatment will probably improve through research, but the treatments that doctors use now are very helpful. The disease may not be curable, but patients can certainly be helped a lot.

GLOSSARY

Anemia *(a-NEE-me-a).* A condition of the blood in which there are not enough red blood cells.

Ankylosing spondylitis *(ANK-a-LO-sing SPON-da-LIE-tiss).* Literally, it means "stiffening arthritis of the spine," and that is what it is.

Antibiotic *(AN-tie-by-AH-tick).* A type of drug used to fight infection caused by harmful bacteria.

Antibodies *(AN-tee-BOD-eez).* Special proteins made by the immune system to defend the body against things that should not be in the body.

Bacteria *(back-TEER-ee-a).* Microscopic organisms, some of which are harmful and can cause infection. Other bacteria are harmless or even helpful to the body. The singular form is bacterium. "Germ" is often used to mean bacterium.

Bursa *(BER-sa).* A little sac, near a joint, that lets muscles slide smoothly over bones and tendons.

Biopsy *(BY-op-see).* A way to diagnose a disease, by taking a tiny piece of tissue out of the body and looking at it under a microscope.

Cartilage *(KAR-til-ij).* A pad that covers and cushions the ends of the bones in a joint.

Corticosteroids *(kor-ti-ko-STEER-oidz).* A class of powerful anti-inflammatory drugs. They have serious side effects so other types of anti-inflammatory drugs are more often used.

Gonococcus *(GON-o-KAHK-uss).* The bacterium that causes gonorrhea. It sometimes causes infectious arthritis in young women.

Gout *(GOWT)*. A form of arthritis caused by crystals of uric acid in the joint.

Hemophilus *(he-MA-fill-us)*. A bacterium that often causes infection, including joint infection, in children.

Immune system *(im-YOON)*. A complex system that defends the body. The defense is called immunity.

Inflammation *(IN-fla-MAY-shun)*. Redness, swelling, warmth, and pain. See Chapter One.

Ligament *(LIG-a-ment)*. A tough cord that connects the bones in a joint to give the joint strength. It works with the rest of the joint capsule to hold the joint together. Compare to *tendon*.

Lupus *(LOOP-us)*. A complex disease caused by antibodies working against the body's own tissues. Arthritis is often a feature of the disease. The full name is systemic lupus erythematosus (ER-a-THEE-ma-TOE-sis).

Osteoarthritis *(OSS-tee-o-arth-RIE-tiss)*. A common form of arthritis caused by breakdown of cartilage. See Chapter Three.

Prostaglandins *(PROSS-ta-GLAN-dinz)*. Complex substances formed when cells are damaged. Certain types of prostaglandins trigger pain by making the nerves in the damaged area very sensitive.

Pseudogout *(SOO-do-gowt)*. Similar to gout, but the crystals are made of calcium pyrophosphate.

Psoriasis *(saw-RYE-a-sis)*. A skin disease sometimes related to a form of arthritis called psoriatic (SAW-ree-AT-ick) arthritis.

Rheumatoid arthritis *(ROO-ma-toid)*. A common form of arthritis that causes inflammation of the synovium. See Chapter Four.

Spondylitis See *ankylosing spondylitis*.

Staphylococcus *(STAFF-ill-o-KAHK-uss)*. A bacterium that can cause infectious arthritis. Often called "staph" for short.

Syndrome *(SIN-drome)*. A combination of problems that happen together. For example, Reiter's syndrome has three problems: arthritis, an inflammation in the eye, and an inflammation in the penis.

Synovium *(si-NO-vee-um)*. The lining inside the joint capsule. Synovial fluid is made by the synovium.

Tendon *(TEN-din)*. A tough cord that connects a muscle to a bone. Compare to *ligament*.

Tophi *(TOE-fie)*. Hard, painful deposits of uric acid in the skin, seen in people who have had gout for many years.

INDEX

Juvenile rheumatoid arthritis, 32

Kidneys, 40, 48
Knees, 16
    infectious arthritis and, 34
    joint replacement for, 51
    osteoarthritis and, 25, 27
    psoriasis and, 40
    Reiter's syndrome and, 43
    rheumatoid arthritis and,
    32-33
Knuckles, *see* Fingers

Laboratory tests, 43, 46-48
Lifestyle, 8, 10
Ligaments, 16, 20-21
    ankylosing spondylitis and,
    38
    contracted, 25
    rheumatoid arthritis and, 32
Lungs, 32-33, 40
Lupus, 40-41, 46, 48

Malaria, 50
Markers, 30, 32, 43, 46
Marrow, 14, 21
Mechanical joints, 51, 53, 56
Medications, 38, 49-51, 54-56
Methotrexate, 51
Minerals, 14, 54
Muscles, 13-15, 20-21
    exercise and, 54
    rheumatoid arthritis and,
    32-33
    weakened, 25

Nervous system, 32-33, 40
Nodules, 43
Nonsteroidal anti-inflammatory
    drugs (NSAID), 50
Nutrients, 23
Nutrition, 54-55

Operations, 51, 56
Osteoarthritis, 22-28, 43
    X-ray of, 47
Osteoarthrosis, 22
Overweight, 27, 54, 56
Oxygen, 23, 54

Pain
    osteoarthritis and, 27
    relieving, 49-50
Penicillamine, 50
Phosphorus, 14
Physical examination, 43
Plasma, 48
Prostaglandins, 8, 49-50
Proteins, 23, 27
    antibodies, 30
Pseudogout, 36, 46, 50
Psoriasis, 40
Psoriatic arthritis, 40
    treatment, 51
Pus, 34-35

Quacks, 54-56

Rash, 40, 43
Red blood cells, 46, 48
Reiter's syndrome, 38, 43
    treatment, 51
Research, 56
Rest, 54
Rheumatism, 8, 29
Rheumatoid arthritis, 29-33, 40
    lab tests for, 46, 48
    symptoms of, 42-43
    tiredness and, 54
    treatment, 51
    X-ray of, 45
Rheumatoid factor, 30, 46

Sedimentation rate, 48

ABOUT
THE AUTHOR

Steven Tiger is a graduate of Brooklyn College and the Physician
Assistant Program of Touro College, New York City. Formerly in clinical
practice as a physician assistant, he has been editing and writing for
numerous medical journals and is also a guest lecturer in medical
physiology at the Physician Assistant Program, The Brooklyn
Hospital / Long Island University. He is the author of *Heart Disease*
in the Understanding Disease series.